Nana's

Beverly Wright

Nana's Very Precious Grandchildren

iUniverse books may be ordered through booksellers or by contacting:

iUniverse
1663 Liberty Drive
Bloomington, IN 47403
www.iuniverse.com
844-349-9409

ISBN: 978-1-6632-4269-3 (sc)
ISBN: 978-1-6632-4270-9 (e)

Library of Congress Control Number: 2022913479

Print information available on the last page.

iUniverse rev. date: 07/22/2022

Nana's

Making Quality Time

Beverly Wright

Acknowledgment

I would like to express my heartfelt love and gratitude towards my Creator, my Lord and my Redeemer, for He is my Everything, and without Him I am nothing! I know that my Dearest Mother, Louvenia Maxine Wright (The Original Nana) is looking down and smiling on me and my siblings, her grands, great grands and all of the rest of our lineage here in this life who loves her, misses her, but welcomes her loving, ever guiding and ever protecting Spirit. God Bless all of those and their families who have helped me along the way in a challenging, sometimes turbulent but yet a productively experience gaining single parenting life. They all know who they are. Too many to list! Without such giving and uplifting support, sincere passion for helping, sacrifice and considerations, I would likely not have grown into the Nana that was there at times for the ones who needed me. I am grateful to Mr. Mark Sussman of Page Publishing with whom I began my journey there. With Mark, I found comfort and assurance that my time and experiences with Page would be unforgettable and rewarding! Thanks bunches to Casey and Andrew who has promptly followed up with any and all of my concerns, that I may have had in the itinerary process, and even Sibilia, who made sure all was well with me from her department.

Introduction

Hello, my young people of today. Allow me to tell you all that "Nana" is a title of honor and respect given to a child's maternal or paternal grandmother. If you would like to come to understand it's origin and literal meaning, I challenge you to research it so that you will get the satisfactory answers of your own personal interest and beliefs!

This fresh and original story is sent from my heart to yours, little ones and young adults to remind you that you do have some adult(s) in your life who really really care about you and your well being, and that they prove it in many ways, mostly when they make the sacrifices that puts you first and them last. If we were to just try to live by that example set for us, it would be easier to love one another, understand one another, get along with one another and be kind and helpful to one another. That's a sure recipe for the world baking into a better "Cake!" Lol!

Do you agree that some days when we wake up that we feel totally great and just want to get right on up and start our day full of joy and happiness, and then there are those days when our high hopes for the day are low and we just want to roll on over, pull the pillow and blankets back over our heads and just to be left alone for a while? On a day like this, I usually close my eyes and think about my Nana and all of the joy and comfort she brought to my life. I would imagine the strength and courage I had always believed that was in her as the top member of my family. I began to feel better already, as I knew she'd be more proud of than to have me feeling sorry for myself. "Poor me, why do I have to get up if I don't feel like it?!!" "Awww maaann, how come I have to get up and do chores?!!" Nana would never give in to those awful feelings. She would beat those feelings down with the strength and courage of Wonder Woman, spring right on up from out of her warm comfort zone of a cozy bed and begin her day with a skip to her step and a song in her heart. Try it! See if it works for you.

Last, but not least, FYI: Grandparent's Day is now a national holiday and is on the calendar for September 9, 2018 this year. A special day set aside to honor our parent's parents, giving us all a chance to show them just how much we care about them! Boys and Girls, on one of these great days ahead of you in your "On the right track" bright future, you may become a grandparent yourself. It will be then that you will benefit abundantly from the fine examples set by your very own. You will easily come to understand why along with the interesting, time consuming, sometimes complex task of running this ole' world, you'll need to also carve out some loving quality and quantities of your very precious time for your "Very Precious Grandchildren."

Boys and girls, there are some gifts in life that are free. They usually are the best ones to get. They are also often the best ones to give. Family, for instance--their love for you and their support of you when you pick and choose things that you may want to try to do in your life is a good example of some of life's best gifts. You can see that these types of feelings are generally thought of as gifts because they come from the heart of a soul and do not have to be given but they are.

Random acts of kindness from adults, such as helping an elderly person across to the other side of the street or helping them get bags of groceries inside their homes is considered a gift to the person or people that they have given their time, extended their helpfulness, kindness and also their consideration to. Taking out the family trash without being asked by someone your age or older could be considered as a gift because you didn't have to volunteer your time, helpfulness, and consideration, but you did anyway just because you love your family and because you wanted to do the right thing without having to be told to.

Everything we do and all that we strive for when we wake up and climb from out of our beds revolves around time. Does that mean that time taken or time given to the day or to each other could be considered a gift? Just as sure as you're born, it could be and often purposely is. Adults all around the globe from all different types of cultures value time in different ways, and most of them have different beliefs and reasons for how and why they give their time to the day or each other. In all of these very large areas and cultures, there is one thing that is agreed upon by everyone. Time consists of two parts, which make it possible for most who are old enough to understand the difference better able to decide what their day is going to be like. Those two parts are quantity and quality.

Grandparents sometimes struggle with choosing between the two parts of time, and some of them even try their best to accomplish both when it comes to this extension of their own children. This is a story about a very happy and peaceful grandmother from a small town somewhere in New Jersey, and she was as happy as she could be. Though they all lived far away, she was grateful and constantly excited to have grandchildren to love.

8

This happy and peaceful lady from NJ who lived a good distance away from her grandchildren wanted to spend some time with them doing certain things that would create precious memories of what she believed to be quality time spent with them. Talking to them on the phone was pleasing to her and made her smile and laugh at some of the things she heard them saying and things she was able to find out that they were doing. Shopping for them and mailing out cards or packages on birthdays and other special occasions gave her great joy. Even talking to her own children, which were their parents about the their growth and changes in their mindsets and behavior as they got older was quite interesting and a gift of love this lady adored and felt privileged to possess. Keeping up with a quantity of loving efforts wasn't quite fulfilling and left a void in this lady's life about her time not spent in person with her grandchildren.

She went by the title of Nana to her grandchildren, and they loved calling her that. She felt warm and fuzzy feelings inside to hear them call her by that title. It was one that was passed down from her own mother. "Hi, Nana" was music to her ears from on the other end of a telephone line, but nothing could replace a face-to-face with her cherished and precious babies. You see boys and girls, all of the grandchildren were of ages whereas by human standards they were no longer considered babies, but to Nana they would always be her babies.

Three of her grandchildren had lived in the great state of Virginia at one point in time, and it was then that Nana was able to give of herself in the scope of a gift of love that she believed could be measured as quality time. She had two darling granddaughters belonging to her son and daughter-in-law-that would soon need someone special to care for them while her children were at the hospital to have delivered and bring safely home the new baby brother that would make the third child to arrive in this wonderful family of hers. Nana knew what she needed to do as soon as she was given the news of a new arrival from the stork. She didn't hesitate to pack up her bags, and Nana moved from NJ to VA to help her children.

The move was a success. The living arraignments were peaceful and rewarding because she got to see her granddaughters daily and even to participate in some of their extracurricular activities from their school. And most of all, her void of absenteeism from quality time in some of her grandchildren's lives was filled. One day as she sat in the living room waiting for the two little princesses that she adored so much to come through the front door from their day at school, she got quite a pleasant and unsuspected surprise from the youngest of them. "Nana, want to see our new cheer?" shouted one of her granddaughters, barely all the way through the front door from off of the school bus. By instinct, she was already bent over with one arm extended upward and the other outward in front of her, striking a cute little cheerleading pose before Nana could answer yes or no! Could Nana had ever seen such an exhibition of love or shared the excitement of that given moment with her granddaughter showing off her little cheerleading skills from over a telephone? Of course not! We know that for certain.

Personal experiences of all kinds captured memories of the quality time Nana purposely spent with her grandchildren. With parents who were happy to have Nana on board for the delivery of the new bouncing baby boy who arrived on schedule, I might add, and also as a quality live-in sitter for the girls during this time, all needs were being met for everyone concerned, but even good things must come to an end. It was time for Nana to return to her own home in NJ, and she did. She was sure to have plenty to write about in her journal that she kept on hand for recording some of the moments of her life to which she could go back and read about in the future, long after the moments had become only mental photographs in her head. Being there for the birth of her second grandson and watching her granddaughters up close and personal was a delight that brought her much joy and much material for her journal. Nana was able to experience joys and angers, victories and upsets, highs and lows, ups and downs, likes and dislikes, beliefs and disbeliefs, as well as growth in mannerisms and behaviors; and she was thrilled to be able to witness it all firsthand.

Once settled back into her usual environment at home, Nana began to experience some of those same old emotions of absenteeism and missing out on quality time with her grandchildren because of living such a long geographical distance from all of them. How come a move to another state didn't fix that problem in Nana's life? I really don't believe that it was the return home that caused the emotional problem to come rushing back front and center right into Nana's awareness as much as it was the fact that she had one other grandchild to care about. She had older grandsons besides the newborn she left behind in Virginia. What is she to do to resolve these feelings that are always creeping up on her? Sometimes at the most inconvenient times like when she's out and about for the day trying to take care of her own household needs. Nagging feelings of missing out on their young and impressionable years of growth seem to slow down Nana's ability to focus. Especially at times when she's constantly seeing images of things remembered from her visit with her grandchildren or from the times they had visited with her. She would ride past a home with little children in a wading pool and automatically think of the time her two girls splashed around in the one she bought them that summer she kept them for a while to give Mom and Dad a break.

Maybe her routine would get interrupted by the site of a basketball court at the end of someone's driveway as the image caused her to gaze and think of some of the games played by her deliciously bright little grandson who lives in South Jersey. She has been looking forward to attending some of them for a while now and has yet to make it. Distance, in addition to scheduled dates and times, have always been the barriers in between Nana and her ability to make it to her grandson's games. "What could she do to fix that?" She would think to herself. By now she had become completely preoccupied with daunting thoughts of how she could satisfy her grandbabies and herself by creating the quality time solutions she was so proud of. Nana's current household task at hand would sometimes suffer quality time because of these vivid distractions. They would sometimes cause her to be late for the things that she had in mind to do for the day.

Nana from Central New Jersey had just about enough of worrying about her last grandchildren whom she felt she had not dedicated enough quality time to as she had done for the granddaughters and their new baby brother in VA. You can bet that she set out to do something to change that. What was on her mind? What measures would she take? What lengths would she go to in order to make things right? How would she go about spreading the quality time efforts around so that all of her grandchildren would have experienced their fair share of her unconditional love? Do you think that she would consider another temporary move to her other son's home to be there in person witnessing and discovering a lot of the developmental stages of her other grandsons? Or would she decide it more doable to keep them at her home for a few weeks of their summer break as she had done with her granddaughters one time before? If she decided to move closer to her grandsons' hometown, what would she do about her future medical appointments that she had with her family doctor, which she had come to love and trust with her and her daughter's life? The distance that would need to be traveled to come back to the office would be too much on both of them.

Nana tossed and turned that night, wrestling with what seemed to be a certain defeat of her choice to relocate. There were other specialist, dentist, podiatrist, optometrist, and such that could take the place of their current doctors, but giving up the warm and personal bond of a family MD is where she would draw the line. The next morning when Nana started her day, she decided that she was still faced with seeking solutions to the absenteeism and lack of quality time in her grandchildren's lives. At the moment she was about to feel sad and defeated, she discovered a piece of mail on the kitchen floor that her daughter had dropped from the rest she had brought in from out of their mailbox the day before. Something at her doctor's office was brewing that would affect Nana's and her daughter's life, and she had no clue until she open the letter. As she unfolded the letter and read what it said, she could not believe what she was reading!

From the Desk of Dr. Nina Barrett-Schott. The letter went on to read as follows:

As I have built my reputation upon services provided and have gained the love and trust of my community residents, I've learned some things from you too while providing for you what I have been noted for, personal and quality health care. It is with my greatest sympathy and deepest regret that I must inform you of an occurrence in my life that will affect most if not all of you in continuing on as my patients.

Recently my husband, one of the Surgeons at our local hospital has been offered a head position at a hospital down in the southern part of NJ. This will be a bittersweet transition from Central NJ to the southern area; because while we will be losing you we will be gaining the joy of family closeness and more quality time will be able to be spent with them. Our children will be able to grow up with and become close with a lot of their cousins!

This move will take place within the next month and you all can be certain that my replacement will be as caring, medically efficient and trustworthy as myself. In the meantime, feel free to pay me a visit before I go.

Riiiiiingg

29

"*Ring*! *Rrriiiiinngg*!" Nana was in her kitchen making dinner for her and her youngest daughter still at home when a phone call came in from her son in South Jersey. A smile as bright as the sun came to her joyful face when she heard who it was on the other end of the line. A striking thought had come to her in the form of a solution that she had struggled to achieve in her attempt get a good night's sleep last evening! "Just touching base," he spoke and said to her--a ritual that he and his siblings would practice faithfully in order to be assured that their dear mother was okay.

"All is well here" is the words in which she would generally use to comfort them. "I've decided to come down there this weekend and look around for a place to live, what areas near your home do you suggest?" she asked him. To her surprise and amazement, he answered without skipping a beat in his voice as if he was undoubtedly able to contain the joy of hearing the good news! She and his baby sister would be moving to his area down in South New Jersey. She was tickled pink to listen to her son express his emotions as if it was a perfectly normal occurrence for someone's mom to announce from out of nowhere that she was soon to be their neighbor. She knew full well that deep inside he was doing somersaults! How grand it would be for Nana to finally be able to attend some if not most of her grandsons' sports activities, not to mention watching them grow into fine young men? Quality time from a beloved grandparent while they are still capable of giving it, needless to say, is a valued and priceless treasure that all grandchildren throughout the world need and deserve!

Quality Time Is Priceless

Some grandmothers make apple,
cherry, peach, or blueberry pies
Some make clothes on their sewing
machines for girls and guys
Some make quilts, sweaters, booties, and hats
While some make room for their dogs or their cats
Some make time for sending prayers up above
Some make gestures, which are filled with love
All of these things and more are the best
When quality time is put to the test
Some will endure, but some will not bother
Some will depend upon Mother or Father
But the best kind of grandparents a child could adore
Is one willing to even the "quality time" score!

About the Author

Beverly Wright was born in Long Brach New Jersey to Robert and Louvenia M. Wright and blessed to be loved and raised by her mother and a loving stepfather, Mr. Henry Walker. She was 8th of 9 children in her family. From the beginning, she needed to learn patience, tolerance, sharing and caring, but most importantly of all she needed to quickly adapt to respecting authority since she had to do as she was told by siblings older than her when her parents were away at work.

Her school years in the Monroe Township educational system was filled with learning herself and people as well as the 3 R's. Life presented something new and fascinating to her at each grade level. Her fifth grade teacher, Mr. Etch was also Mayor of the little rural town, and Beverly even shared him and his generous guiding affections with his daughter Janet as her classmate. Beverly and her sibling's bus driver, the very nice and complacent Mr. McCarthy was the same driver every year, so she was given the opportunity to learn the personas of different titles of people in her life.

Today you will find that she is home with her daughter Zakira, who is a young adult born with Downs Syndrome, nurturing and caring for her daily needs. Being home with Zakira has given this author the wherewithal to use her free time in developing her writing skills. She loves children and believes that special needs children are sent to special people in the cosmic scope of life as it is.

Beverly's biggest aspiration concerning her entry into the world of literary expressions is for her messages to evoke a burning desire in grownups to respect and protect our children. She considers them our future.

Printed in the United States
by Baker & Taylor Publisher Services